ALL KINDS OF
EARS

Sara Swan Miller

Benchmark
New York

Marshall Cavendish Benchmark
99 White Plains Road
Tarrytown, New York 10591-9001
www.marshallcavendish.us

All Web sites were available and accurate when this book was sent to press.

Editor: Doug Sanders
Publisher: Michelle Bisson
Art Director: Anahid Hamparian
Series Designer: Alex Ferrari

Library of Congress Cataloging-in-Publication Data

Miller, Sara Swan.
  Ears / by Sara Swan Miller.
      p. cm. — (All kinds of ...)
  Summary: "An exploration of animals ears, their various shapes and
functions"—Provided by publisher.
  Includes bibliographical references (p. 47) and index.
  ISBN-13: 978-0-7614-2518-2
  1. Ear—Juvenile literature. I. Title. II. Series.

  QL948.M57 2007
  591.4'4—dc22

                              2006019712

Photo research by Anne Burns Images

Cover photo: Corbis/Joe McDonald

The photographs in this book are provided by permission and through the courtesy of: *Corbis:* Kevin Schafer, 1; Jim Cummins, 4; Micro Discovery, 6; Brandon D. Cole, 20; Michael & Patricia Fogden, 22; Lynda Richardson, 24; Clive Druett, 27; ER Productions, 30; Roger Wilmshurst/Frank Lane Picture Agency, 34; Jeremy Hardie/zefa, 35; Frans Lemmens/zefa, 38; Stuart Westmorland, 43; Jim Craigmyle, 45. *Peter Arnold Inc.:* Martin Harvey, 7; Medimagery/The Medical File, 8; J. Brackenbury, 13; Helga Lade/GmbH Germany, 19, 32; R. Andrew Odomi, 29; Fritz Polking, 36; IFA, 41. *Animals Animals:* Patti Murray, 10, 25; David M. Dennis, 12; Bernard Photo Productions, 14; O.S.F., 15; Gregory W. Brown, 16; Gerard Lacz, 18; David M. Dennis, 26; Michael S. Biscegue, 40.

Printed in Malaysia
1 3 5 6 4 2

CONTENTS

Our ears pick up sounds, even if they are muffled underwater.

WHAT ARE EARS ANYWAY?

When you think of ears, what do you picture? Probably you think of ears like yours, on either side of your head. Maybe you picture the long ears of a rabbit, or the pricked-up ears of a German shepherd or a cat. Perhaps you think of an elephant's huge flapping ears or the long drooping ears of a basset hound.

Most mammals have ears, or *pinnae* as they are known, on the outside of their heads. Most of the time, we can see a mammal's ears easily. But mammals are the only animals that have external ears. Can you imagine a bird with ears sticking out? Or a snake? Or a fish? Yet even without ears on the outside, all these animals can hear, some better than you can.

How do your ears work? The outer parts of your ears are great at gathering sounds from the air. The important parts of your ears, however, are found inside your head. The sound waves that your outer ears gather travel down a tube called the *auditory canal*. Next, they hit your eardrum, or *tympanic membrane,* and cause it to vibrate. On the other side of your eardrum are three tiny bones—the *hammer,* the *anvil,* and the *stirrup.* Each

The little bones in a rabbit's ear, called otoliths, are shown here, magnified 1,500 times.

bone looks like what its name suggests. (An anvil is a thick block on which heated metal objects are shaped, while a stirrup holds a person's foot when riding a horse.) The vibrations from the eardrum are picked up by these three bones in your *middle ear,* and they start vibrating too.

The vibrations from the middle ear then pass through a membrane called the *oval window.* Next they travel to the *inner ear,* where a spiral passage called the cochlea is found. It is a fluid-filled structure that looks like a snail shell. The vibrations from the oval window make the fluid inside the cochlea vibrate too. The vibrations bend tiny hairs inside, which send signals to the nerve cells at their base. Then the nerve cells send impulses through the *auditory nerve* to the brain, where they are translated into sounds that you can recognize. All of this happens in a fraction of a second.

We can hear sounds in a range of pitches, or *frequencies.* Sounds travel in waves, and the cycles, or vibrations,

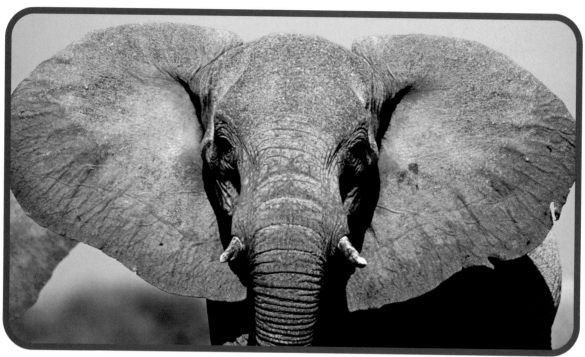

An African elephant stretches its ears out wide to show how angry it is.

are measured in *hertz*. A frequency of 1 hertz, for instance, means that there is one cycle per second. One hertz, of course, is a very low-frequency sound, which we cannot hear. People can hear sounds in a range of 20 to 20,000 hertz. Frequencies that are higher than the ones humans can hear are called *ultrasound*. Frequencies lower than we can hear are called *infrasound*.

There are other structures in our inner ear—the *semi-circular canals*—that have nothing to do with hearing. They are three loop-shaped tubes, each at right angles to the other two. Picture the back, legs, and arms of a chair. The semicircular

I HEAR YOU!

People can best hear frequencies from 1,500 to 4,000 hertz. That is the frequency range of human speech.

canals are in similar positions. They give us our sense of balance. The canals are filled with fluid and lined with sensitive hair cells. When you move your head, the fluid rocks inside the semicircular canals and moves the hair cells. Impulses, or signals, travel from the hair cells through a part of the auditory nerve to the areas of your brain called the *medulla* and the *cerebellum*. That way, your brain knows what position your head is in.

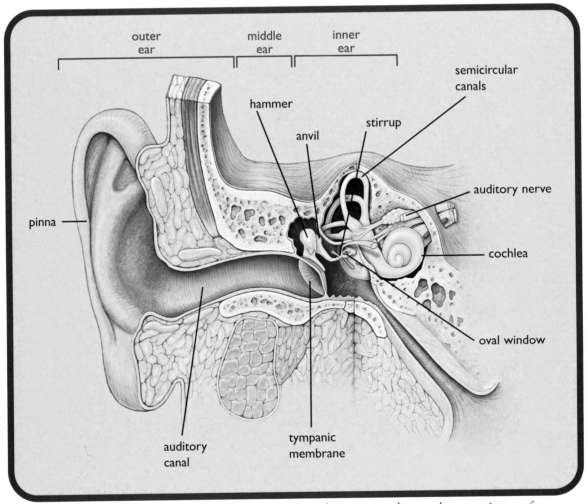

Sounds are gathered by the outer ear, then sent through a variety of structures on their way to the brain.

Have you ever spun around and around until you became dizzy? That feeling is caused by the fluid forced to one end of the semicircular canals. It sends strong impulses to the brain. When you stop spinning, the fluid rushes back the other way and makes you feel as if you are suddenly twirling in the other direction. The awful feeling of car sickness is also caused by the semicircular canals. The movement of the car rocks the fluid in the canals and irritates or bothers the hair cells.

In the animal world, ears come in all shapes and sizes. Each animal group has developed hearing that is best suited to its needs. Hearing helps animals find prey and mates, avoid danger, and communicate with one another, among many other things.

Let's find out more about all kinds of animal ears!

EARS IN ODD PLACES

What is the best place for ears? Your head seems like a good place for them to be—right next to your brain. Many other animals, such as birds and reptiles, also have their ear openings on their head. But some animals, including insects, have their ears in other places, even on their knees.

*Butterflies can sense vibrations
with their wings.*

2

INSECT EARS

Our sense of hearing is very important to us. We use it mostly to communicate with one another, to share thoughts and information. Our sense of hearing can warn us of possible danger, such as a train whistle or the sound of a car racing toward us. Hearing also allows us to enjoy music and birdsong.

While hearing is so important to us, many insects cannot really hear, at least not the way we do. All insects have hairs on their body that pick up vibrations. But most of them do not have eardrums. Some insects, such as some butterflies, can pick up sound vibrations with their wings.

THEY'RE NOT LISTENING

How about other invertebrates, animals without backbones? Can they hear? Not really. Sponges, hydras, and jellyfish are deaf. They use touch and smell to sense the world around them. Anemones, snails, and starfish cannot hear either. Earthworms have no actual sense of hearing, but they do have receptors, special parts that sense touch, light, and vibration all along their bodies. Crabs and crayfish have hairs on their claws and bodies that pick up vibrations in the water, but they cannot actually hear either.

This female mosquito is sampling some human blood. A male can track her by listening to her whirring wings.

A mosquito, however, can hear. Its sense of hearing is not highly developed, though. It has *hair sensilla* attached to its antennas. They are like threads that move easily in the breeze and can pick up low-frequency sounds. Males use their sensilla to find a female. As a female flies, she makes low-frequency sounds with her wings. Males are drawn to the sound and chase after her to mate. A female does not have as good a sense of hearing as the males. After all, when it comes to mosquitoes, it is the male's job to find her.

Most moths do not have eardrums, but there is at least one family that does. Noctuid moths are small and fly at night, so you can guess why some people call them owlet moths. Don't look for an owlet moth's eardrums on its head, though. Oddly enough, its eardrums, called tympana, are on the sides of its body at the end of its *thorax*. The moth has two sound-gathering cells connected to its tympana. These cells can pick up ultrasonic sounds, which are too high for us to hear. An owlet moth's ears help it know when a bat is after it. As a bat flies, it sends out ultra-sonic sounds that bounce off the moth's body. When an owlet moth hears those sounds, it knows a hungry bat is nearby. Quickly, it tries to escape, flitting this way and that.

When you think about crickets and their nighttime chirping, you know they must be able to hear. The males' sounds are their way of calling to their mates, so you know they must have ears. But where are they? The ears are actually found on the front legs. Males call to females by rubbing their jagged front wings together. The females point their knees in the direction of the

A cricket's ears are on its front legs.

EQUAL RIGHTS?

For most insects that sing, it is the males that make the music. Female katydids, however, call just as loudly as males.

A close-up of the ear on a katydid's front leg.

love song. If they recognize the sound as one made by a male of the same species, they hop right over.

You have probably heard katydids calling out on summer nights—"Katydid! Katydid! Katydidn't!" To us it sounds as though they are having a terrible argument. But the katydids are just calling for mates. Like crickets, they make their loud calls by scraping their front wings together. They have eardrums on their front legs, just like crickets.

Grasshoppers also call out to their mates. The males make their calls by drawing their hind legs over the edge of their wings. But where are their ears? They are not on their front legs this time, or on their thorax. Instead they are on the sides of their *abdomen*, toward the front. Look closely at a grasshopper and you may spot the flat, round tympana.

Have you ever heard the loud buzzing of cicadas in the trees on a hot summer day? The males make their mating calls using a *tymbal,* a round membrane on their abdomen connected to muscles. A male moves his tymbals rapidly in and out. This motion creates a series of very loud clicks. The male does it so quickly that the clicking sounds like one long buzz. The female has ears, of course, but they are hard to see. If you could look at a cicada through a magnifying glass, you would find the ears on the sides, on the first part of the abdomen.

An insect's ears are not as complex as ours. The tympana have sensory neurons attached to them, cells that carry messages to the central nervous system. Air sacs around the tympana help magnify or increase the sound as the tympana pick up vibrations. Insects probably do not hear as many different kinds of sounds as we do. Mostly, they have ears just to help them find mates.

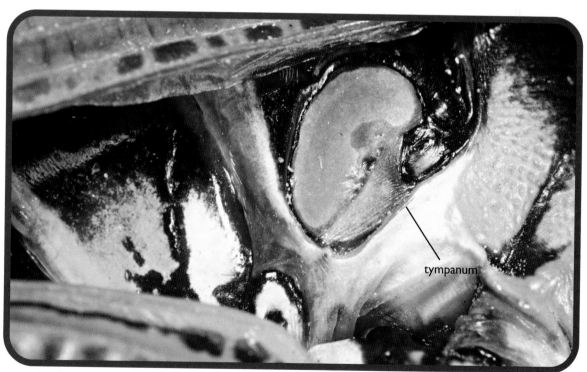

A close-up of a grasshopper's tympanum or eardrum.

A fish's ear hole is hard to spot.

3

ARE THE FISH LISTENING?

If you talk to a fish swimming about in an aquarium, can it hear you? Yes, it can. It doesn't understand what you are saying, of course, but it can detect the sounds you are making. So how can a fish hear? Where are its ears?

Many bony fishes have tiny openings in the skin behind their eyes. These openings lead to their inner ear. But fish use more than their ears to hear. They also have special organs called *lateral lines* on the sides of their body, which are sensitive to water pressure and vibrations. Vibrations can also pass easily through their soft body tissues and make their *swim bladders* and the little bones in their inner ear vibrate. A swim bladder is an air-filled sac that most fish have. It helps keep a resting fish from sinking to the bottom or floating to the surface. The swim bladder also acts as an amplifier, making sounds louder.

Some fish hear much better than others, though. Carp and minnows, for example, have connections between their ears and swim bladders that help them hear very well. This connection is known as the *Weberian apparatus* and is made up of tiny bones. When the bones vibrate, the sound waves are passed on to the inner ear.

Minnows can sense vibrations and water pressure using their lateral lines.

Inside the inner ear is a curled structure call the *labyrinth*. It is filled with fluid, which moves and jiggles in time to the vibrations. Tiny hair cells inside the labyrinth pick up the vibrations and send the signals to the brain.

Like us, fish have semicircular canals in their inner ears, filled with fluid. When a fish swims about, the fluid moves around and comes in contact with the nerve cells. This is how fish know which way they are swimming and how they are able to gain a sense of speed and direction. Spinning quickly around can make a fish dizzy, just as it can with humans. The fluid sloshing about tells the fish's brain that it is spinning, but its other senses tell it that it is holding still.

How well do fish hear? Sound travels about 4½ times faster through water than through air, because water is

DIZZY SHARKS

Sharks can get dizzy just as we can. Something especially odd happens when a shark is turned upside down. The shark gets confused by the messages sent from its semicircular canals. Instead of righting itself by flipping over, the shark just lies there. It won't move until it is turned right side up again.

denser. This greater speed means that fish can hear sounds traveling from far away. Most sharks, for instance, can pick up sound vibrations from as far away as 150 feet (50 meters). Some can hear over even greater distances. A shark's strong sense of hearing, along with its excellent sense of smell, help it close in on its prey. It is hard to hide from a shark!

Some fishes, including shad and herring, can hear ultrasonic noises. Most fishes hear sounds in the range of 20 to 800 hertz. (Remember, we hear sounds from 20 to 20,000 hertz.) But they can also hear sounds from 25,000 to

A gray reef shark can hear sounds coming from far away.

180,000 hertz.) Being able to hear high-pitched sounds helps these fishes escape from hungry dolphins. Dolphins send out a series of high-pitched sounds that bounce off their fish prey. By using sound in this way, dolphins can locate where a possible meal is. But shad can hear these sounds and race far away from danger.

Fish use their sense of hearing to communicate with one another. Some fishes make sounds by grating their teeth. Others, such as catfish, can also use their air-filled swim bladders to make grunting sounds. They

Male midshipmen fish make incredibly loud noises when calling to their mates.

use these sounds to call for a mate and to gather in groups called schools.

Some fishes make incredibly loud noises at mating time. The fish called midshipmen that live off the west coast of North America are especially loud. The males use their swim bladders to make a humming noise that sounds like a group of motorboats. People who live nearby can find it hard to sleep during mating season.

The males hide in caves while they call to the females. It is the female's job to find them. How does she find one mate in all the racket? The female is able to pick out one special signal that she is interested in. She follows the sound right into the male's cave and lays all her eggs for him to fertilize. After that, she is done laying eggs for the season, but the male keeps on humming away. One by one, more females pick up his signal and lay their eggs.

It may seem surprising that fish can hear so well without having their ears on the outside. But there is more to fish ears than meets the eye!

A caecilian can sense
vibrations in the water.

CAN A FROG HEAR?
CAN A SNAKE?

How well do amphibians and reptiles hear? That depends on which kind you are talking about. Some hear quite well, but others are nearly deaf.

Caecilians, for instance, are little-known amphibians that look like large worms. They live underground or in the water. They find their way through the dark mostly by touch and smell, so they don't really need to hear very well. They don't have ear openings, eardrums, or middle ears. But they do have inner ears, which have hair cells inside that send signals to the brain. Even without ear holes, in water or mud caecilians can sense low-frequency vibrations. How is that possible? The skin and muscles on their head pick up the vibrations and pass them along. On land, however, caecilians are deaf.

Salamanders are similar to caecilians, but their hearing is a bit more like ours. They, too, have no ear hole, eardrum, or middle ear. But they have a more complex inner ear, which can sense low-frequency sounds. When a salamander hears something, the vibrations go

Silent salamanders sense vibrations, but do not hear very well.

through the oval membrane on one side, through the fluid in the brain, and out the oval membrane on the other side. In one ear and out the other!

Salamanders that live in the water also have lateral lines, as fish do. They can sense water pressure and some vibrations, so the salamanders know when prey or predators are near. Salamanders that live on land can pick up vibrations from the ground with their toes. Because salamanders do not use sounds to communicate with one another, they do not really need to hear well. Most salamanders are silent, except for a few that make little popping or squeaking sounds. Males and females find one another mostly by smell.

Frogs, however, are a whole different matter. You have probably heard frogs calling for their mates in the spring and summer. You can't miss the trilling of tree frogs, the GUNK! of a green frog, or the deep twang of a bullfrog. Each kind of frog has a different mating call, and the females manage to find the right male despite all the racket. A good sense of hearing is very important to frogs.

It is easy to find a frog's eardrums. Its large round

tympana are right behind its big goggly eyes. When the eardrum picks up vibrations, they pass into the middle ear and make the little bones found there vibrate. Those vibrations travel into the inner ear, where there is a complex system of sensory areas and nerve cells. They pass the information on to the frog's brain.

Male frogs hear as well as females. They can tell whether another frog's call is a mating call to draw or attract a female or a territorial call meant to drive other males away.

Unlike frogs, turtles don't hear very well. They do not have ears on the outside of their bodies to gather sounds, and their eardrums are covered with skin. But they do have inner ears, so they can pick up lower

THE FROGS ARE LISTENING

Frogs can also hear when a storm is coming. Frogs that live in the desert often burrow underground during the hot, dry summer. When they hear thunder rolling and rain falling above, they know it is time to come out again. Frogs can hear people coming too. Even if you creep up quietly, a frog will hear you and leap with a splash into the safety of the water.

A green frog has very large ears.

frequencies. Hearing is not key to the lives and survival of turtles and tortoises. Most of them don't communicate using sounds. Some species make little noises while mating, while some tortoises grunt quietly when they are courting a mate. But mostly they are mute. Turtles make up for their poor hearing with their excellent senses of smell and vision.

Alligators, on the other hand, hear very well. It is not surprising, then, that they make so many different calls. Some species have more than twenty different messages to share with one another. When courting a mate, for instance, the males bellow loudly. When alligators sense danger, they cough and hiss. Hatching baby alligators make high piping calls, and when the babies are in trouble they make sharp distress calls. Those are just a few of the things that alligators and crocodiles have to say.

Can you find an alligator's eardrums? They are just behind its eyes near the top of its head. Scaly, movable flaps of skin protect the eardrums when an alligator is underwater. Because its ears are near the top of its head, an alligator can stay almost entirely underwater and still be able

A hatching alligator makes little sounds its mother can hear.

to hear what is going on around it. An alligator's middle ears and inner ears are well developed—the better to listen for the many different messages alligators have to share with one another.

Look on the sides of a lizard's head and you can probably see small ear openings behind its eyes. Just inside those ear openings are the lizard's eardrums, which send sound vibrations to its middle and inner ears. Some lizards don't have middle ears, but their inner ears can pick up low-frequency sounds. Most lizards hear quite well. They are alert to the sounds of danger and the movements of prey.

Even though lizards have a good sense of hearing, most are quiet. Only a few can be noisy. Geckos, especially, can make a lot of different sounds. Some only squeak, but a tokay gecko barks loudly or makes a warning growl when it is frightened. Some geckos call to attract mates, as frogs do.

A male tokay gecko calls loudly to attract a mate.

Each species has a different call, and females, with their good hearing, can pick out the sound of just the right mate.

Have you ever seen a picture of a snake charmer playing his pipe while a snake bobs and "dances" to the music? It looks as though the snake is enjoying the tune, but it is not actually dancing at all. What it is really doing is keeping its eyes on the flashing pipe swaying back and forth, as the snake gets ready to strike.

Snakes do not have ear holes, as most lizards do. So for years scientists thought snakes could not hear much at all. But now some scientists think that may not be the case and that snakes hear better than once thought.

SOUND IN THE GROUND

As it glides along, a snake uses its jaws to pick up sound vibrations traveling through the ground. Solid material transmits or moves sound along much better than air. Maybe you have seen a western film where the skillful Indian guide lays his ear to the ground to hear if the bad guys are coming. You can try a similar experiment to see how well sound travels through solid material. Hold a wooden yardstick to your ear and ask a friend to place a ticking watch on the other end. How well can you hear the ticking? Now ask your friend to keep holding the watch where it was, but take away the yardstick. How well can you hear the ticking now?

You can try yet another experiment to see how well sound travels through water. Take a long tube-shaped balloon and fill it with water. Hold it to your ear and try the same ticking watch experiment you did with the yardstick.

Inside a snake's head there is a bone called the quadrate. A snake picks up sound vibrations through its skin and muscles. These pulses are sent to the quadrate, then to a bone called a *columella,* and finally to the cochlea.

Whatever we might think of a snake's hearing, a snake will definitely be able to hear you if you speak in a deep voice. Snakes can mostly detect low-frequency sounds, such as the sounds of large animals walking along. When a snake hears the sound of a large animal coming, it freezes. Maybe it will not be noticed if it lies still in the brush.

Unlike lizards, snakes have no ear holes.

When you take a nature walk, you can often hear a chorus of birdsong.

WHEN BIRDS LISTEN TO BIRDS

Take a walk in the woods on a spring morning, and you'll hear birds everywhere. "CHEER! CHEER! CHEER!" "CHICK-A-DEE-DEE-DEE!" "WICK-WICK-WICK!" Birds are loudly calling to their mates and defending their territory or home area against strangers. Clearly, being able to hear must be important to these noisy creatures.

Beside vision, hearing is a bird's most valuable sense. In dense woodlands, especially, where it is hard to see through the trees, birds need to stay in touch with one another by calling and listening. Many woodland birds have especially loud calls to communicate with other members of their species.

Birds do not have ears on the outside of their heads, of course, but other than that their ears are a lot like our own. Birds have ear holes on the sides of their heads, which are hidden under the feathers. Sound vibrations enter the holes, travel down the auditory canal, and strike the eardrum. The sound vibrations are made stronger by the eardrum and then pass into the middle ear. Inside, a bird has just one little bone, not three as we do. This single ear bone, the columella, sends the vibrations to the cochlea and other structures in the inner ear. Nerve cells in the cochlea then relay the information to the brain. Like us, birds also have semicircular canals in their inner ears that help them with balance and moving about. This is especially important to birds as they fly and swoop through the air.

Birds hear sounds much as we do. They hear sounds best in more or less the same range as people—about 2,000 to 4,000 hertz. That is why birdsong is so easy for us to hear and so useful in identifying birds at a distance. Birds do not hear lower frequencies—those less than 100

Birds rely on their strong sense of hearing to communicate with one another.

hertz—as well as we do, though. Some birds can hear frequencies up to 29,000 hertz, but others, such as mallard ducks, have a much smaller range, from 300 to 8,000 hertz.

Despite the things we have in common, a bird's sense of hearing is different from ours in some ways. For one thing, birds can hear much briefer sounds than we can. Humans can hear separate sounds about $1/20$ of a second long. Birds can hear sounds that last only $1/200$ of a second. So, while we may hear just one sound, a bird might hear ten separate notes.

If you have ever seen a long-eared owl, you might be asking, "Don't some owls have external ears?" Those "ears" are just tufts of feathers on top of the owl's head. They have nothing to do with its sense of hearing. Mostly they act as camouflage when an owl is sitting on a branch near a tree trunk. The tufts on its head help the owl blend in and look like a branch.

Owls have an excellent sense of hearing, though. Their saucer-shaped faces act like a satellite dish, catching sounds from the air the way our ears do. Inside their head most owls have asymmetrical ears. That means one ear is lower than the other. Sound vibrations from a scurrying mouse reach one ear before the other, so the owl can pinpoint the exact location of its prey. An owl can hear the squeak of a mouse $1/2$ mile (0.8 kilometers) away.

The "ears" of this long-eared owl are actually just tufts of feathers.

Some birds use echolocation, as bats do. The oilbirds of South America live in dark caves and only come out at night to find food. They send out bursts of sound

that echo off the cave walls and help them find their way in the dark. Echolocation also helps them avoid crashing into trees when they fly away from the cave. But they probably do not use echolocation to find their food. Unlike most bats, which eat insects, oilbirds eat hanging fruit, so they rely on their other senses to locate it.

Calling and hearing are important to birds all their lives. Some birds even start calling when they are still in their eggs. Unhatched quail babies, for instance, make little piping sounds that both their mother and the other chicks can hear. Listening to one another, the quail chicks can plan a group hatching and usually shed their shells within two hours.

Unhatched chicks also listen to their mothers

Quail babies talk to one another even before they hatch.

I CAN'T HEAR YOU

Hearing is so important to birds that a deaf mother turkey does not recognize her young at all.

from inside the egg. A mother mallard duck, for instance, calls to the chicks while she is sitting on the eggs. When they hatch, they already recognize their mother's voice and flock to her. Knowing their mother's voice is especially important to young birds that live in colonies. With so much squawking going on at once, a baby bird can find its own parents and beg for food from the only ones out of hundreds of birds that will feed it.

Birds in big colonies also need a strong sense of hearing to find their mates. Emperor penguins, for instance, live in big, noisy colonies. A female may be off

Emperor penguins can recognize their mate's voice out of hundreds of others.

hunting fish in the ocean for weeks, while the male sits on the egg. When she returns to the colony, she calls loudly. He answers back until she finds him in the crowd.

Birds rely on their sense of hearing in many different ways. They listen to one another's songs in courtship and to help them stay together in a flock. Parents and young recognize one another mostly through sounds. Birds listen for danger and send out loud warning calls when they sense trouble. Birds depend on their ears. Among other things, ears help make a quick escape possible.

*A fennec fox's big ears swivel
around to capture sounds.*

6

MARVELOUS MAMMAL EARS

Like their early ancestors, most mammals are nocturnal or active at night. As a result, they have developed an excellent sense of hearing.

Over millions of years, mammal ears have evolved or changed in some marvelous ways. Look at the huge ears of the little fennec fox. Those big ears can catch the slightest sound, and the fox can swivel them to catch sounds from all directions. Fennec foxes can even hear a rodent burrowing under the sand or the high-pitched squeak of a tiny insect underground. They are always on the alert for danger too. It is hard to sneak up on a fennec fox!

Fennec foxes live in the desert, and their large ears give off a lot of heat and help the foxes stay cool. In the cold nights, the foxes flatten their ears to keep heat in. Foxes that live in cold places, such as the arctic fox, have smaller ears that do not give off a lot of precious body heat.

Many kinds of mammals, especially the ones that live in hot places, have large ears. Think of jackrabbits, elephants, kangaroos, aardvarks, deer, antelopes, and hyenas. All of these mammals have excellent hearing.

Like many mammals that live in hot places, hyenas have large ears that help the animals release body heat.

They can use their ears to cool off in hot weather as well. Elephants also use their ears as fans. The hotter it gets, the faster they flap them. Like the arctic fox, mammals that live in cold places have small ears.

Some mammals use their ears for more than just hearing. Many of them communicate with one another using their ears. For instance, a wolf points its ears forward when it is alert and listening or when it is happy to see another member of the pack. When it is scared, it lays its ears down flat. If another wolf threatens it, it will lay its ears down and turn the insides forward—a way of returning the threat.

Some mammals' ears are specially adapted to their environment and the way they live. A camel, for instance, commonly found in the desert with its fierce sandstorms, has ears lined with hairs that keep the sand from blowing in. Beavers, which spend time both on land and in the water, have ears well suited to their lifestyle. On land they prick up their ears to listen for predators. But when they dive into the water, they close off their ears, which keeps the liquid out.

You probably know that bats use echolocation to zero in on their prey. As they fly along, they send out high-pitched beeping sounds. These beeps bounce back when they hit an object and tell the bat exactly where its insect prey is. A bat may send out twenty-eight beeps a second. It moves its ears rapidly to catch the echoes.

Other mammals also use echolocation to find their prey. Shrews, for instance,

AMAZING ECHOLOCATION

A bat can fly 60 miles (97 kilometers) per hour, using echolocation to find a moth on even the darkest of nights.

The ears of a long-eared brown bat help it pick up tiny sounds when it hunts for insects.

SEAL EARS

Seals—and their ears—are well adapted to life in the ocean. When seals dive, the channels to their eardrums are closed off by water pressure. A pocket of air trapped inside picks up vibrations from the seawater, so seals have excellent hearing.

send out high-pitched clicks that bounce off their insect prey in the darkness. Besides helping the shrew find its dinner, the clicks may confuse its prey and make it easier to catch.

All land mammals have ears that stick out of their heads. But where are a whale's ears? Or a dolphin's or an elephant seal's? All of these mammals have ear holes and no external ears. Big ears would just get in the way of mammals that spend most of their time swimming underwater. They need a sleek shape to their body and head to help them swim quickly. They also have narrow auditory canals and small thick eardrums that keep water from getting into their middle ear.

There is a long list of earless marine mammals. Manatees, dugongs, whales, porpoises, dolphins, and walruses are just a few. Sea lions are an exception. They do not spend as much time in the water as other marine mammals, and they have little ears on their heads to show for it.

You might think that without ears on the outside, these marine mammals do not hear very well. Actually, they have a good sense of hearing. A whale or a seal swimming along in murky water needs to be able to hear well to find its way and to track down prey. As you have learned, sound travels much better through water than through the air, so marine mammals can hear noises from far away. Whales, for instance, can communicate with one another over hundreds of miles. They can also hear ultra-sound and infrasound that we cannot detect at all.

Sea lions are one of few marine mammals that have external ears.

If you look closely at a dolphin's ears, you can see tiny openings just behind its eyes. What you can't see is the dolphin's well-developed auditory nerve. It has twice as many nerve fibers as our auditory nerves do, which means a dolphin can pick up sounds much better than we can. Sounds are sent to a dolphin's middle ear mostly through its blubber and its lower jaw. Blubber is mostly fat, and a dolphin's lower jaw is filled with fatty tissues. Fat conducts or relays sounds very well, so a dolphin can hear sounds we cannot. It can hear high-frequency tones from 75 to 150,000 hertz, while we only hear sounds up to 20,000 hertz.

Like bats, dolphins use echolocation to find their prey. They send out blasts of high-pitched clicks that are repeated many times a second. When the sounds bounce off a school of fish, a dolphin can then head in its direction. Other marine mammals, including toothed whales, also use echolocation. But baleen whales, which feed on tiny creatures called krill, do not need echolocation. Neither do manatees, which feed on water plants.

Do other mammals hear better than we do? Some, such as sloths, have less complex ears and do not hear very well. But many mammals have a much better sense of hearing than we do. Elephants, for instance, communicate with one another using rumblings that are too low for us to hear. Cats, on the other hand, can hear high-pitched squeals that are beyond the range of our hearing. Dogs, too, can hear high-pitched whistles that our ears are unable to detect. All dogs, especially the ones with pointy ears, have much better hearing than we do. You can see how they cock their head to locate the source of a dog can hear a thunderstorm coming from miles away.

Rodents also hear much better than we can. A kangaroo rat, for instance, can hear the faint sound of an owl gliding overhead. We can only hear an owl flying when the sound is made louder using special equipment. Kangaroo rats can also hear the tiny sound a snake makes just before it strikes, which we cannot detect at all.

It is hard to imagine what the world sounds like to rodents, dogs, cats, elephants, bats, and all the other mammals that hear things we cannot. Mammal ears are marvelous!

A dog can hear high-pitched whistles than people cannot.

45

GLOSSARY

abdomen—The third and last segment of an insect's body.

anvil—A small bone in the middle ear that picks up vibrations.

auditory canal—A tube that carries sound waves to the eardrum.

auditory nerve—A part of the ear that sends sound information from the cochlea to the brain.

cerebellum—A part of the brain involved in muscle coordination and balance.

cochlea—A fluid-filled spiral structure located in the inner ear.

columella—A bone inside a bird's middle ear that picks up vibrations.

frequency—The number of waves per second produced by a sound source.

hair sensilla—Threadlike structures on a mosquito's antennas that pick up sounds.

hammer—A small bone in the middle ear that picks up vibrations.

hertz—A unit of frequency equal to one cycle, or vibration, per second.

infrasound—Frequencies lower than we can hear.

inner ear—An area between the middle ear and the auditory nerve that contains the cochlea.

labyrinth—A curled structure inside a fish's inner ear that picks up vibrations.

lateral lines—Sensory structures on a fish's sides that are sensitive to water pressure and vibrations.

medulla—An area deep within the brain.

middle ear—The area between the eardrum and the oval window.

oval window—A membrane between the middle ear and the inner ear.

pinna—The name for the outer, visible ear on a mammal's head; plural, *pinnae*.

quadrate—A bone in a snake's head that sends vibrations to the cochlea.

semicircular canals—Fluid-filled loop-shaped tubes in the inner ear that provide a sense of balance.

stirrup—A small bone in the middle ear that picks up vibrations.

swim bladder—An air-filled structure in a fish's body that keeps it from rising or sinking in the water.

thorax—The second of three segments of an insect's body.

tymbal—A round membrane on a cicada's abdomen that creates a buzzing sound.

tympanic membrane—Another name for the eardrum.

ultrasound—Frequencies higher than we can hear.

Weberian apparatus—A structure made up of tiny bones connecting a fish's ear and swim bladder.

FIND OUT MORE

BOOKS

Barre, Michel. *Animal Senses*. Milwaukee, WI: Gareth Stevens, 1998.

Cerfolli, Fulvio. *Adapting to the Environment*. Austin, TX: Raintree Steck-Vaughn, 1999.

Gamlin, Linda. *Eyewitness: Evolution*. New York: Dorling Kindersley, 2000.

Hickman, Pamela, and Pat Stephens. *Animal Senses: How Animals See, Hear, Taste, Smell, and Feel*. Buffalo, NY: Kids Can Press, 1998.

Kalman, Bobbie, and Jacqueline Langille. *How Do Animals Adapt?* New York: Crabtree Publishers, 2000.

Parker, Steve. *Adaptation*. Chicago, IL: Heinemann Library, 2001.

Santa Fe Writers Group. *Bizarre and Beautiful Ears*. Santa Fe, NM: John Muir Publications, 1993.

ORGANIZATIONS AND WEB SITES

The Animal Diversity Web
http://animaldiversity.ummz.umich.edu/site/index.htm
This site contains information about individual species in several different groups of animals, particularly mammals.

Audubon Society
http://www.audubon.org
This organization is an amazing source of information for people interested in birds and bird-watching.

Cyber School—Marine Life
http://ourworld.compuserve.com/Homepages/jaap/Mmlinks.htm
This site provides information on many fishes and other marine life.

Insect Inspecta World
http://www.insecta-inspecta.com
This site has all kinds of information about insects.

Neuroscience for Kids—Amazing Animal Senses
http://faculty.washington.edu/chudler/amaze.html
At this site, you can learn a lot of amazing facts about animal senses.

INDEX

Page numbers for illustrations are in **boldface**.

ABOUT THE AUTHOR

Sara Swan Miller has enjoyed working with children all her life, first as a Montessori nursery school teacher and later as an outdoor environmental educator at the Mohonk Preserve in New Paltz, New York. As director of the school program, she has taught hundreds of children the importance of appreciating the natural world.

She has written more than fifty books, including *Three Stories You Can Read to Your Dog; Three Stories You Can Read to Your Cat; Three More Stories You Can Read to Your Dog; Three More Stories You Can Read to Your Cat; Three Stories You Can Read to Your Teddy Bear; Will You Sting Me? Will You Bite? The Truth about Some Scary-looking Insects;* and *What's in the Woods? An Outdoor Activity Book.* She has also written many nonfiction books for children.